£5.75

contents

INTRODUCING OASIS   6

MOSS SIDE STORY   8

LIAM FACT FILE   14

HOLD THE FRONT PAGE   16

TRACKS THAT CHANGED THE WORLD   20

NOEL FACT FILE   24

THE DIRTY DOZEN   26

I WRITE THE SONGS   30

BONEHEAD FACT FILE   32

SOME MIGHT SAY   34

JUST FOR THE RECORD   38

GUIGSY FACT FILE   40

GREATEST SHOWS ON EARTH   42

BOYS IN THE BAND   46

OASIS SUPERQUIZ   48

ALAN WHITE FACT FILE   52

MAD FOR IT!   54

BIGGER THAN THE BEATLES?   58

© 1997 Grandreams Limited

Published by
Grandreams Limited
435-437 Edgware Road
Little Venice
London W2 1TH

Written by Mick St Michael and Ian Welch
Layout and design by Simon Joslin
Photographs supplied by All Action

Printed in Belgium

INTRODU
OASIS

If the 1990s was the Brit-pop decade, then Oasis are surely the men of the moment. The famous five from Manchester – well, four and a Cockney drummer, as Noel might say – have made their home city famous for producing great musicians as well as fantasy footballers. And the music they've made has not only topped charts worldwide, it's transcended all labels, rooted in the melody of the 1960s while remaining as fresh and contemporary as the milk on your doorstep.

Yet all this didn't spring fully formed from nowhere. The living, beating heart of the band is the relationship between brothers Liam and Noel Gallagher, singer and songwriter respectively, backed up by the most muscular three-man rhythm section you'll find outside a demolition gang. The combination of talent, technique and tub-thumping power is now nothing less than legendary.

Between the covers of this book you'll find many of the secrets that have fuelled their meteoric rise to the top. Is Liam *really* as bad as he's painted? What does the rest of the pop world think of them? Which of their many releases were the groundbreakers, and why? And, last but not least, will they eventually be bigger than their heroes, the Beatles?

Burning questions one and all…and ones we're happy to answer here. In this world of uncertainties, one thing's for sure. As long as Oasis produce the kind of music they've given us in the past five years, there'll be many millions hanging on their every note!

MOSS SIDE STORY

Well Burnage, to be absolutely accurate. But there's no doubt that the Manchester suburbs gave birth to an extraordinary band. Here's how it happened...

It's now something of a cliché that visitors to Manchester in winter comment on how often it rains. The joke's somewhat lost on the city's inhabitants – but if Mancunians could loosen up for a while, we can explain that the Oasis story begins with rain – a band called Rain. And very suitably, given future events, the outfit took their name from a Beatles song.

Rain had been formed by guitarist Paul 'Bonehead' Arthurs and bassist Paul McGuigan, known to one and all as Guigsy, who recalls their first meeting. 'It was in a pub one night. Bonehead said he wanted to be in a band – he could play piano and guitar – I said "that's amazing, I wish I could", and he said "you can play the bass, you only have to play the top string." That's how it started.'

Together with drummer Tony McCarroll and a singer whose name history does not record, the duo played mostly covers of pop and punk classics, including the Troggs' 'Wild Thing'. But things didn't start moving until Liam Gallagher, the youngest of three brothers brought up in the grey, unglamorous suburb of Burnage, auditioned to become their new vocalist.

Having failed to impress at school, he'd been faced with the dole queue but had already, according to his mother Peggy, 'spent hours locked away in his bedroom, determined to sing himself to stardom'. The only job he'd ever held down was as a car valeter, polishing flash motors, but after he'd applied those talents to his singing he would prove to be the jewel in Rain's crown.

Noel Gallagher, five years older than Liam, was an interested observer in a crowd of about 20 as the new quartet made their first appearance at the Boardwalk club in Manchester. As a former roadie for the Inspiral Carpets, he knew all about the rock'n'roll lifestyle and was hungry for more. Though he later claimed Rain had been the worst band he'd ever seen in his life, he had a proposition for them. 'I've been writing songs for years. Let me join on lead guitar. I'll write the songs and everything'll be rosy.' He did – and it was!

Noel's debut gig with Rain, now renamed Oasis after a trendy clothes shop, was at the Boardwalk on 19 October 1991. The crowd by now had doubled to 40 people, and the newly augmented outfit unveiled their original material with pride. Sadly, in Noel's words, the Fab Five 'went down like a knackered lift…in silence. We thought they were going to be in raptures!'

Undeterred, Oasis licked their wounds and made the short journey down the East Lancs Road to Liverpool, where they recorded a demo tape of Noel's songs: even then, classics like 'Married With Children' and 'Columbia' that would later become world-famous were in the repertoire. Local label Factory Records turned them down, denying them the chance to be labelmates with New Order and Happy Mondays – so perhaps it should come as no surprise that they were

9

discovered not in Manchester but Glasgow, where they played as support to 18 Wheeler in May 1993.

Creation Records' boss Alan McGee had come along to see the headliners, and was intrigued by rumours of a 'Scouse Sex Pistols'. He takes up the tale: 'There were 15 kids from Manchester all sitting round a table and one kid in plain white Adidas looked like Paul Weller. I had no idea that this was Liam Gallagher. Sure enough, the band came on with this kid as the front man…he was so confrontational that you just thought, God, he's really got attitude.'

Things got even better, so by the time the set had climaxed with an Oasis-ised version of the Beatles' 'I Am The Walrus' McGee had nothing else on his mind but signing the boys to a record deal – double quick!

Oasis's debut single, 'Supersonic' only reached Number 31 in the national charts,

but live appearances were already becoming semi-legendary. So too was their off-stage misbehaviour, which came to a head while travelling on a cross-Channel ferry. The incident in which all but Noel ended up 'in the brig' may not have had anything much to do with music, but did succeed in turning the name of Oasis into

national press headlines. And by the time of their next single, Oasis were indisputably the Next Big Thing.

'Shakermaker' gave them their first major hit, stalling just one place short of the all-hallowed Top 10 in June. But an unfortunate similarity to the New Seekers' 1971 chart-topper 'I'd Like To Teach The World To Sing' resulted in having to share some of the royalties. (Ironically in 1996 an Oasis tribute band, No Way Sis, would cut a version of the Seekers song…Liam-style!)

After a third single, 'Live Forever', the stage was set for the release of an album. Titled 'Definitely Maybe', it had proved painfully slow to come together, having been recorded in no fewer than seven studios – yet its speed out of record-shop doors would become legendary. Indeed, sales of 100,000 copies within a week won it the accolade of the fastest-selling debut album in indie rock history.

Next came a promotional visit to the States, where the band played at an event called the New Music Seminar and left the assembled music-business VIPs in no doubt that they weren't about to conform to their rules. No-one was arguing, since memories were still warm of an on-stage riot in Newcastle, where an audience member had invaded the stage and hit Noel in the face. 'We're here to play songs,' Liam had explained, 'but if someone gets up and thinks he's a bit hard and goes for it, he's going to get it.'

'Cigarettes & Alcohol' and 'Whatever' ended 1994 with two more hits – but the press were keen to compare the band with their 'Cockney counterparts', Blur. A war of words would ensue that made the friendly 1960s rivalry between the Beatles and Rolling Stones look like handbags at 12 paces. The first shots were fired at *New Musical Express*' prestigious Brit Awards in

January 1995, where Liam flatly refused to pose with Blur's Damon for a photo – even though it would have more or less guaranteed them a cover story. And that wasn't the end of it…

It was a major shock when Tony McCarroll, the band's original drummer, parted company with the other four. Not only was it against the 'street gang' philosophy that had served Oasis so well so far, but an album's worth of material lay waiting to record. Noel, though, had heard something he perceived as musical weakness, and nothing would be allowed to compromise his vision for the band. Though Tony drummed on the first single, the rest of the album would be entrusted to Alan White, a top session man whose brother Steve was Paul Weller's permanent percussionist.

The long-running Brit-pop 'feud' came to a very public head in August when Oasis's latest release 'Roll With It' coincided with Blur's new single, 'Country House'. Unfortunately for Noel, his statement that Blur were a bunch of middle-class kids 'trying to play hardball with a bunch of working-class heroes' fell rather flat when Blur took the top spot. Consolation came in October with the release of '(What's The Story) Morning Glory?', which did even better than its record-breaking predecessor by selling 350,000 copies in a week and hogging the Number 1 spot in numerous countries.

The pressure was all too much for Guigsy, who stepped down for a US tour – but was back in the ranks as Oasis prepared for two nights at London's Earl's Court in November, an engagement hailed as the biggest indoor concerts ever in the UK. With tongue in cheek, Oasis selected the Bootleg Beatles tribute band as their opening act, and there were distinct traces of the Fab Four's influence in the headliners' new single, 'Wonderwall'. Nor was the fun over yet: the Creation Records Christmas party had more surprises in store, notably a piano for Bonehead and a Rolls Royce for Noel – who, ironically, had yet to pass his driving test!

As 1996 opened, the band were back in the singles chart at Number 1 with 'Morning Glory's third single, 'Don't Look Back In Anger', which included a stage favourite in Slade's 'Cum On Feel The Noize'. Ex-Slade singer Noddy Holder returned the compliment by showing up at Manchester City's Maine Road ground for one of two April gigs by the band that kicked off a summer of outdoor fun.

Liam's high-profile relationship with Patsy Kensit, discussed in detail elsewhere in this book, was the factor that kept Oasis in the headlines in 1996 after the mega-gigs finished. Because, instead of going off to the States to promote their second album, he decided not to board the plane – 15 minutes before take-off time. Creation Records suggested the laryngitis that had kept him from singing at a London MTV Unplugged show meant he wouldn't have appeared in the first show anyway.

Though Liam rejoined the rest of the band in Detroit, he then walked out and the tour was eventually called off completely.

The official word put problems down to 'internal differences', with rumours of the brothers coming to blows. But far from sounding off at his brother Noel had, initially at least, been sympathetic to a fault. 'You have to support people who are going through a personal crisis. So no, I don't feel like slapping Liam.' Rumours of a split abounded, but a later statement made it clear that Oasis would continue as a band and would be releasing their long-awaited third album in 1997. It was clear the Moss Side – sorry, Burnage – story still had a few more twists and turns to come...

FACT FILE:

LIAM GALLAGHER

BIRTHDATE:
21 September 1972

BIRTHPLACE:
Burnage, Manchester

STARSIGN:
Virgo

DISTINGUISHING FEATURE:
Snarl, occasional beard

NICKNAME:
Our Kid

INSTRUMENTS:
Vocals, tambourine

PREVIOUS EXPERIENCE:
Lead singer with Rain

INFLUENCES AND IDOLS:
The Beatles, Stone Roses, John Lennon

THE PRICE OF FAME:
Some of fame's fun, some of it's not fun.
It's 50-50.'

FAVOURITE SAYING:
Mad for It!

LEGENDARY FOR:
Swearing at photographers

BIGGEST HEADLINE:
Missing the plane for a US tour/not getting
married to Patsy Kensit

IF OASIS ENDED TOMORROW...
He'd turn to films and make a million in
Hollywood

QUOTE UNQUOTE:
We're the future of music, never mind just
rock, pal. I hope someone comes along and
tries to take our crown, though – it'd be nice
to have a bit of competition. If we're meant to
be the new Beatles then where are the new
Stones and the new Who?'

4

LIAM

100%
UNOFFICIAL

15

HOLD THE FRONT

There's always been a thin line between truth and rumour as far as Oasis are concerned. Their relationship with the press has been one that's changed rapidly over the years. Having at first been grateful for any media coverage they could attract, the love affair swiftly turned sour as the boys found themselves followed by long lenses every time they set foot outside their own front door. The number of pictures that exist of scowls, V-signs and worse suggest it's something the Gallaghers are mad at, not mad *for*...

Pressure's something you learn to live with – but given the Gallagher brothers' reputation as hot-heads (deserved or otherwise) and the non-stop appetite for news driven by the tabloids, satellite TV and a whole raft of new radio stations, the media spotlight in the 1990s is several times brighter than anything the Beatles, for instance, had to live with.

Liam's responded to the attentions of Fleet Street's finest by laying some fascinating false trails. In 1995, he fooled *The Sun* with the story that he was to wed, and had proposed to his so-called 'girlfriend' at the Glastonbury Festival. He's also made no secret of the fact that he fancies Justine Frischmann from Elastica...though part of the attraction was undoubtedly the fact that her off-stage partner is Damon Albarn, lead singer of rivals Blur.

The biggest headlines concerning his love life came in February 1997 – and this time, believe it or not, Liam was more or less innocent! The tabloids, and even breakfast TV programmes, had got it into

heir heads that he was about to become
he third 'Mr Kensit', and were staking out
his home. The Sunday papers had
mpressions of the clothes the happy couple
would wear, media person Mariella
Frostrup was lined up to be chief
bridesmaid and every detail of the
ceremony had been planned out with
ntricate detail. Trouble was, it wasn't going
o happen!

PAGE

Even when the 'bride' and 'groom'
didn't show, the papers wouldn't leave it
alone: next month's story suggested they
were going off to marry on Gibraltar…
which happened to be where John Lennon
and Yoko Ono got spliced back in
1969. The pair did outwit the media,
however, holding a secret wedding in early
April 1997.

Not all Oasis' headlines, of course, have
been totally without foundation. The
infamous ferry incident, for instance, was
undoubtedly an occasion where they lived
up to their billing as the Wild Men of Rock.
Liam's solo activities have also brought
headlines, notably when he started a
November 1996 evening at the Groucho
Club in London's fashionable Soho and
ended the night in a police station.

The Battle of Brit-Pop back in 1995 gave
the papers a field day. Did Blur *really* bring
the release date of their single forward to
compete with Oasis? We may never know!
Noel expressed it in his usual succinct way:
'I really don't think Blur and us would have
gone into the charts at 1 and 2 if it hadn't
been for the press building it up into such
a big battle. It sells issues, doesn't it?'

Liam's walkout on the eve of the band's
1996 American tour got them in the
opinion columns of the *Daily Telegraph*, no
less, which thundered on about the
declining standards of today's stars in
relation to behaving badly. 'Where is the
appetite for hell-raising displayed by, say,
Jim Morrison and Keith Moon and other
stars of the 1960s and 1970s?' it
complained. 'Liam Gallagher is just 23 and
already he is settling down. They don't,'
the paper concluded sadly, 'make them like
they used to.'

Fascinatingly, while the so-called 'Wibbling rivalry' of Liam and Noel has been well documented, there have been comparatively few stories about the band splitting up for good. The problems that cropped up in recording that all-important third album made good copy in November 1996, *The Sun* exclaiming 'Oasis Quit Abbey Road In A Fury'. Funny, we thought it was a limousine…

With a General Election looming in 1997, Oasis were making the political pages as well as the music press. 'The Night New Labour Found Oasis' was the headline over a story explaining how, after meeting at the previous year's Brit Awards, prospective Prime Minister Tony Blair and Noel Gallagher had become mutual admirers. With Damon Albarn also called upon to give Labour clues to capturing the youth vote, there looked like being a showdown at Number 10 should both sides of the 'think tank' ever get to meet behind that famous door!

It's amazing how many Oasis headlines have been puns on song titles. Plenty of Looking Back In Anger, Maker Shakers (in *Melody Maker*, where else?) Tragical History Tours (the Beatles, but who's quibbling?) and Supersonic Youths. Perhaps the best came from *Top Of The Pops* magazine where Noel revealed the secret that would shake a nation. 'I love Liam, but not as much as I love Pot Noodles.'

Yes, whichever way you look at it Oasis have been a gift to the nation's newspapers. And while yesterday's news is tomorrow's fish and chip paper, you can more or less guarantee that the five men from Manchester – and two in particular – will remain in the media spotlight for as long as they choose to make records.

TRACKS THAT CHANG THE

Oasis have created so many classics it's almost impossible to pick out their greatest hits. But here are eight tracks we've highlighted as making the biggest impact.

SUPERSONIC

The first the world heard of Oasis was on 11 April 1994 when their first single, 'Supersonic', was released by Creation. The song, writer Noel recalls, 'just came out of nowhere…I knew it was a classic as soon as we'd finished.' Few people realise that 'Supersonic' appeared the same week as Nirvana mainman Kurt Cobain's death hit the headlines. You could say that this was the month Seattle gave way to Manchester, but Oasis' initial success was, in chart terms at least, more solid than meteoric as the record reached Number 31. A live appearance singing 'Supersonic' on TV's *The Word* confirmed it was worth more than that, though, and the very next gig left 200 disappointed punters on the pavement as 'sold out' notices were posted. They've never failed to fill a British venue since.

There has been much discussion and debate in the music press about the identity of the mysterious Elsa mentioned in the lyrics. Noel later revealed she was 'a nine-stone Rottweiler dog which was in the studio where we were recording.'

Not that it mattered – this was classic rock that let the world know in no uncertain terms that there was a supergroup in their midst.

LIVE FOREVER

Having made such an impact with their live performances, it was only a matter of time before Oasis exploded into the Top 10 – and 'Live Forever' was the song that did the trick in August 1994. It would also prove a key track on the band's first album that rapidly followed it into the racks.

'People said to me after "Live Forever", "where are you gonna go after that?" Noel recalls. 'I said I didn't think it was that good…I think I can do better.' That said, he recalls playing it to the band on an acoustic guitar was 'one of the greatest moments I've ever had as a songwriter.'

Though he didn't write it, Liam's the man who sings it – and every time he does he thinks of ex-Beatle John Lennon, who died tragically in 1980. '"Live Forever" – if you get to know yourself, and you get to know your spirit, your spirit will live forever. John Lennon is living now, living out there, living in everybody who's into the Beatles. He's living in me – simple as that.' So this is the song that affirms the connection between Oasis and the Beatles.

WHATEVER

Everybody wants a Christmas chart-topper. And though 'Whatever', released in December 1994, didn't turn out to be it – it was just too late – it did give Oasis their very first Top 3 single the following month.

It's notable too in being a single big enough to fill the gap between albums, appearing neither on 'Definitely Maybe' nor its successor. Historically it was one of the first songs Noel wrote and had been specially reserved for such an occasion.

ED WORLD

SOME MIGHT SAY

Every band no matter how big remembers their first Number 1 – and Oasis are no exception. Released in April 1995, 'Some Might Say' entered the chart at the very top, just as the split with drummer Tony McCarroll was announced.

Its sudden appearance knocked fellow Mancunians Take That off the top – and this for Noel 'proves we've done everything we said we would. It's as much a success for our fans as it is for us.'

A classic in anyone's book, the song very nearly didn't become a single at all, having been slated as Oasis's contribution to the 'Help' album put together to raise funds for child refugees in Bosnia.

Noel would link with Paul McCartney and Paul Weller instead for the cause. Yet had the song appeared on that worthy collection, it wouldn't have been out of place, containing some thought-provoking lyrics.

'The verses are quite deep,' Noel revealed. 'Some of them are about homeless people, and people who can't always get what they want, and how people who can get what they want always seem to be moaning more than people who can't.' Some might say he had a point…

WONDERWALL

The October 1995 release of 'Wonderwall' was no surprise, being one of the standout tracks on the just-released '(What's The Story) Morning Glory?' album. What was unusual, though, was the fact it only reached Number 2, being held off the top by Robson and Jerome. The video was great too and fully deserved the Brit award it earned in '96.

Noel wrote the song about his girlfriend Meg, who was out of work and feeling a bit sorry for herself at the time. 'It's just saying, "Cheer up and get on with it!",' he laughed. His brother didn't rate the song at first, but now terms it 'the greatest song ever written!'

Note, too, the sly Beatles reference as the drums come in on the word 'backbeat' – one of many subtleties the Mike Flowers Pops missed when they did their easy-listening version.

Noel, who was amused by that, was less keen on the Smurfs doing a cover, and refused them permission – a decision every right-thinking music lover will surely applaud!

'I always knew it would be a hit,' he said, 'but I think anyone who heard it could have told you that.'

It was one of the songs Noel thinks got nearest to the Beatles blueprint, and he had confirmation of its classic status when Paul McCartney named it as one of his favourites. 'I went round his house in St John's Wood one night. He liked "Slide Away", "Whatever" and "Live Forever". If I'd been knocked over by a taxi that night, I'd have died the happiest man.'

ROLL WITH IT

Released in August 1995, this was the song that competed with Blur's 'Country House' in the Battle of Brit-pop – and even though it was beaten to Number 1 the following week is still one of the greats.

'It's just a typical Oasis thing,' says Noel dismissively: 'Shut up moaning and get on with it. You've gotta say what you say, and be who you be.' Is it about Liam? Apparently not. 'They're just words that come out, none of them are about anything really. We just thought it was a good song for the summer.'

'Roll With It' was the first track Alan White recorded with the band. 'It's got a little sparkle. I did a few others which are a bit more solid. But with that one, everyone was moving with one another and it sounds good as a band.'

DON'T LOOK BACK IN ANGER

Sung by Noel, this was the single that took revenge on Blur in February 1996 by going straight in at Number 1, leaving 'Stereotypes' to flounder in its wake. Unusually, Bonehead was playing piano on the record, having been given the instrument as a thank-you by the record company for his part in Oasis's success.

The video featured Patrick MacNee, alias Steed from 1960s TV classic *The Avengers*, and in a mocking sideways glance at Blur was shot at a big house – a very big house – in the country!

The chorus mentions a girl called Sally, but Noel claimed not to know anybody of that name. 'It was just a word that fitted, and I thought, "Y'know, might as well throw a girl's name in there".'

Like many Oasis songs it was a rallying cry to forget about past problems and look to the future. 'Today's another day and tomorrow's the day you've got to dream of. Don't look back in anger if anything in your life has gone wrong.' Not bad philosophy.

THE NEXT SINGLE

With Oasis, the best is always yet to come. Noel had originally intended 'My Big Mouth' to be the first single off the band's third album, the working title of which was 'Be Here Now', but he was so spoilt for choice as the release date approached that he confessed he'd changed his mind. Recording had been completed by March 1997. 'Liam's got to sing a couple of songs, I've got to put down a few more guitar riffs, and that's it.'

Describing the new LP, he said it was like a 'heavy rock album, basically. It's rocking, but it's not innovative. There's no new ideas going on. It's just us. It's just Oasis playing guitars. It's more good songs. Really good songs.' The musical ingredients were said to include string sections, sampling and drum loops – maybe a legacy of Noel's work with the Chemical Brothers.

FACT FILE:

NOEL

100%
UNOFFICIAL

NOEL GALLAGHER

BIRTHDATE:
29 May 1967

BIRTHPLACE:
Burnage, Manchester

STARSIGN:
Gemini

DISTINGUISHING FEATURE:
Broad grin (when thinking of songwriting royalties)

NICKNAME:
Has been compared to Parker from _Thunderbirds_

INSTRUMENTS:
Guitar

PREVIOUS EXPERIENCE:
Roadied for Manchester band the Inspiral Carpets

INFLUENCES AND IDOLS:
The Beatles, Paul Weller, Steve Jones, Johnny Marr

THE PRICE OF FAME:
Claims getting stopped in the street for an autograph is the best feeling in the world.

FAVOURITE SAYING:
Top!

BIGGEST HEADLINE:
Threatening to dump Liam when he didn't turn up for a TV show

IF OASIS ENDED TOMORROW…
He'd become an in-demand songwriter and producer

QUOTE UNQUOTE:
'I remember my mum sitting me down one night and saying, "What is going to become of you?" and I didn't have an answer. But she never once told me to get a proper job or settle down and get married. She just used to say, "You'd better not let me down," and I've not.'

THEDIRTY

1 Noel walked out of the studio while Oasis were recording 'Definitely Maybe' to teach the others a lesson. 'We'd put six tracks down, I was working 18 hours a day at the time and I came back one night and half of Monmouth were in my room. I'm well up for a bit of partying but all these people were there...'

The strangers told Noel that Liam and Bonehead had invited them. 'So I found the others and I said, "We're here to make a record not National Lampoon's *Animal House*. I'm off to Jersey for a couple of weeks, go and sort yourselves out." They freaked out, but I had to remind them that we were working.'

2 People never ask Noel f his autograph, thinking he looks too grumpy to approach. 'What they don't understand,' he laughs, 'is that I *always* look like this!'

3 'Some Might Say' was inspired by 'Ooh La La', an old record by Rod Stewart and the Faces. 'If it hadn't have been Number 1 I'd have been amazed,' said Noel. 'It's a top song. The sleeve's got loads of references to things in the song, although I haven't any idea what any of it means. It's just words that sound good.'

Twelve little-known facts behind Oasis and their success. If you knew all of these, your name is probably Gallagher!

4 In musical terms, Liam proudly claims he lives in the past 'and I think it's top. All my mates are into the Chemical Brothers. I hate it. Non-imaginative keyboard crap. Rock'n'roll will never die.' Oh, Liam – guess who Noel went and recorded a Number 1 single with…?

5 Noel admits he hasn't a clue what makes his brother tick. 'I think he's at war with the world, but I'm not sure why. There's something really getting to him, but I don't know what it is. He's always questioning everything, looking for answers. 'I think life's just a load of questions. If I don't find the answers now, then I'm sure they'll turn up later on. Our kid doesn't want that, he wants to know all the answers right *now*.'

6 If the Gallaghers weren't in a band, Liam reckons they'd be having rows in the house. 'If we had a greengrocers, Gallagher's Greengrocers, we'd argue over which way to set out the apples or pears.'

100% UNOFFICIAL

7 The last two tracks of 'Morning Glory' are actually a concept. Over to Noel: 'You're in a helicopter, and then you get booted out and you parachute down into the set of *Apocalypse Now*, where it's just kickin' off all around you, or maybe an urban scene where there's riots going off, people getting beaten up and looting and fires everywhere. Y'know, street-fighting-man music. Then this tune comes in...'

8 When he finally passes into rock'n'roll heaven, Liam wants a very special tombstone for us to remember him by. 'On my grave, I want them to write, "Don't Come Here With Your Bunches Of Flowers." I don't want a gravestone, I want a V-sign, two fingers, 20 foot tall or something. When you're dead, you're dead. It's now that matters.'

9 Noel borrowed a guitar from ex-Smiths man Johnny Marr, but it got damaged in an on-stage fight. The next day, Marr sent a taxi to the hotel in Leeds where Oasis were staying with a new Les Paul in it. 'There was a note telling me what he'd played on it; "You'll like this one, it's a lot heavier and will fracture anybody's skull if you get a good swing on it..."'

10 Noel gets a lot of his inspiration for new songs while watching TV, his guitar on his knees. He wrote 'Acquiesce', the B-side of 'Some Might Say' and one of Oasis's hardest-to-find classics, while watching the OJ Simpson trial where the title word came up. 'I didn't have a clue what it meant but it sounded a dead good word. It means being dragged into something no matter how you try to resist.'

11 Rock'n'roll stardom has taken Oasis all over the world – but whisper it quietly to British fans, Liam reckons Japan is the best place ever. 'It totally blew my head, and everyone else's. Getting chased round shopping precincts… It was like Hard Day's Night, man. The tour bus is stuffed with presents, loads of records, dead dear Beatles stuff, purple vinyl and that…'

12 He may be a brilliant songwriter, but Noel has one great fear – 'I'm afraid of running dry. Every songwriter is afraid of picking the guitar up and nothing coming out. That's why we keep going. Your most recent song could well be your last. Look at Lee Mavers (of the LAs). I think he got writer's block. That's why I'm going to record four albums before I lose the point, unlike Lee, who only did one. And the Stone Roses didn't do anything for five years.'

I WRITE THE SONGS

'I wrote my first song in my bedroom just to see if I could do it. After that I wrote about 75 songs no-one's ever heard.'

That's how Noel Gallagher explains his introduction to songwriting back in the 1980s. Since first shaking hands with his creative muse, he's set the rock world alight

with some unforgettable anthems. Yet few people realise he had to overcome the handicap of dyslexia or word blindness to get where he is today. 'Anything over six letters and that's me gone,' he laughs. 'Sometimes I give lyrics to Liam and two key words of a sentence will be missing.'

The second stage came when Noel was 20. 'I started playing at parties and they'd go, "Wow. You should be a professional." That got me over the hurdles of playing my songs to other people – nobody actually laughed at me. After that I was out to conquer the world, man.'

The first people he conquered, of course, were the other members of Oasis then playing cover versions under the name of Rain. It was clear they were going nowhere fast by relying on other people's material. By taking on Noel as an extra guitarist they had access to his stockpile of songs, and suddenly people began to sit up and take notice.

It's been claimed that he took over his brother's band, so starting the 'wibbling rivalry' between the siblings that's so caught the headline-writers' imagination. But that's hardly how Noel sees it. 'To be fair to the rest of the band,' he recalls, 'I don't think it was a surrender. Once you've heard a song like "Live Forever"…I remember playing it to them on an acoustic guitar one night, and it's one of the greatest moments I've ever had as a songwriter. They were just completely and utterly speechless. If I hadn't had the songs, they'd probably have told me to **** off.' They didn't of course!

Songwriting not only brings its own rewards – it also gives you the lion's share of the cash, a fact Noel happily admits. 'The advantages are that if you're the songwriter you earn the most money. If you're a band

member then you earn a living.' Against that, of course, is the weight of expectation on his shoulders. Having come up with the songs for two classic albums and a selection of singles, early 1997 saw him under pressure to produce even more – and that having spent many months on the road, in an atmosphere hardly conducive to creativity. Yet the decision to abort an American tour gave him the breathing space to come up with a collection of songs insiders were suggesting would be the best yet.

Though he's happily settled down with long-time girlfriend Meg Matthews, the guitar is Noel's closest friend. And he admits 'If it all ended tomorrow, I'd still write songs because that's what I do. I did it when I was broke and on the dole and, ever since I was 11, playing the guitar has been my only escape.'

We get the feeling that day is a long way off...

100% UNOFFICIAL

FACT FILE
BONEH

PAUL ARTHURS

BIRTHDATE:
23 June 1965

BIRTHPLACE:
Manchester

STARSIGN:
Cancer

DISTINGUISHING FEATURE:
Thinning thatch, serious expression

NICKNAME:
Bonehead

INSTRUMENTS:
Guitar, piano

PREVIOUS EXPERIENCE:
Played with Liam and Guigsy in Rain

INFLUENCES AND IDOLS:
None he lets on about

THE PRICE OF FAME:
None – he's rarely recognised

LEGENDARY FOR:
Looking hard

BIGGEST HEADLINE:
Helping trash the Columbia Hotel

IF OASIS ENDED TOMORROW…
He'd start a recording studio in Manchester with his royalties

QUOTE UNQUOTE:
'I used to be a plasterer, but my heart wasn't in it. I could never see myself still doing it in 30 years' time. No time off now? Tell me about it…It's all great, though, even the travelling, sitting on a bus and having a few beers, that's not bad. Who wants a day off?'

EAD

100%
UNOFFICIAL

"Did I see Oasis? Yeah, I saw them. They were a laugh. They were such a laugh. I couldn't stop laughing. Are they a joke band? Because I just don't get it. The whole thing is over my head, it seems so old-fashioned and ripped off."

**ANDY,
ECHOBELLY DRUMMER**

"I always knew Liam had it in him. While everybody else was working, he'd just go upstairs, put a tape on and go for it. Noel was the same. He could have got a record deal on his own six or seven years ago, but he decided to wait and get a band together. He's glad he did now."

BROTHER PAUL

"We met Oasis backstage at the Brits. I think the songwriter is really talented and I like their music, but when we went over to talk to them, the singer started slaggin' us off. He was going "Who do they think they are? Get them out of here." Our guitarist put his hand under the singer's chin, just to shut him up. Suddenly, about four of their bodyguards were on him. We only wanted to find out what Oasis were like because we'd heard so much about them."

**PORTISHEAD'S
GEOFF BARROW**

"I've been waiting for this group for ten years. They're the best group I've ever worked with."

**CREATION RECORDS BOSS
ALAN McGEE**

"After Take That, I was really depressed. People kept on telling me I wasn't going to make it on my own. Noel's been really supportive. They're a top band – "Cast No Shadow" had the best words. They're definitely an inspiration. Top Band."

**EX-TAKE THAT STAR
ROBBIE WILLIAMS**

SOME MIGHT

> Liam spent hours locked away in his bedroom determined to sing himself to stardom. His idol has always been John Lennon and he and his brother have bought every Beatles record ever made.

MUM PEGGY

> Noel picked it (his Dad's old guitar) up one day and never put it down. He started strumming and took to it immediately. He had an instant knack for it and I could tell he was a natural. I've still got that guitar.

DAD TOM

> I love the band. There's something that happens between a performer and an audience – that moment when something special happens. They're good guys.

SNOOKER STAR ALEX 'HURRICANE' HIGGINS

> I saw them and immediately felt the Oasis effect – a breath of fresh air, genuine quality, energy, all the things I've been hooked on in 20 years of British rock and pop music rolled into one, which hasn't happen for many years.

MANAGER MARCUS RUSSELL

> There'll never be another Beatles, and Oasis shouldn't be compared to them.

JON BON JOVI

100% UNOFFICIAL

SAY

When you're as newsworthy as Oasis, everyone has their point of view about Manchester's finest. Here are just a few of them...

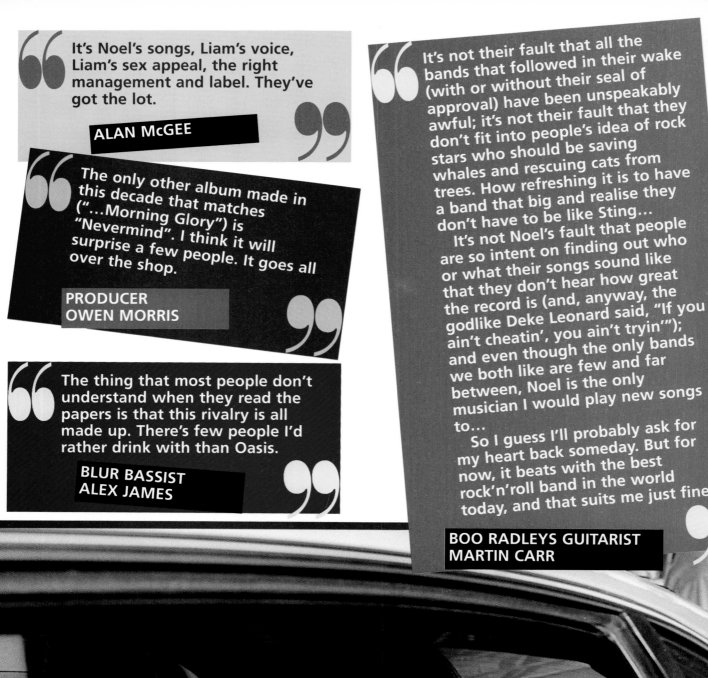

> It's Noel's songs, Liam's voice, Liam's sex appeal, the right management and label. They've got the lot.

ALAN McGEE

> The only other album made in this decade that matches ("...Morning Glory") is "Nevermind". I think it will surprise a few people. It goes all over the shop.

PRODUCER OWEN MORRIS

> The thing that most people don't understand when they read the papers is that this rivalry is all made up. There's few people I'd rather drink with than Oasis.

BLUR BASSIST ALEX JAMES

> It's not their fault that all the bands that followed in their wake (with or without their seal of approval) have been unspeakably awful; it's not their fault that they don't fit into people's idea of rock stars who should be saving whales and rescuing cats from trees. How refreshing it is to have a band that big and realise they don't have to be like Sting...
>
> It's not Noel's fault that people are so intent on finding out who or what their songs sound like that they don't hear how great the record is (and, anyway, the godlike Deke Leonard said, "If you ain't cheatin', you ain't tryin'"); and even though the only bands we both like are few and far between, Noel is the only musician I would play new songs to...
>
> So I guess I'll probably ask for my heart back someday. But for now, it beats with the best rock'n'roll band in the world today, and that suits me just fine.

BOO RADLEYS GUITARIST MARTIN CARR

> Oasis' music is necessarily subversive. Its strength is that oldies like me don't like it. If your parents like the same songs as you, it's because you've bought bad records.

MOVIE DIRECTOR KEN LOACH

> I am God. And Liam is my only son. When that guy sings there is something, there's some sort of ache, as well as the anger, and it's that ache that separates some music from others.

BONO

> I've got one thing to say to Liam – Come and have a go if you think you're hard enough!

SPORTY SPICE AT THE 1997 BRITS

JUST

FOR THE RECORD

The singles and albums that took Oasis to the top

SINGLES

Supersonic/Take Me Away/I Will Believe (live)/Columbia (demo)
Creation CRESCD 176

Shakermaker/D'Yer Wanna Be A Spaceman?/Alive (8-track demo)/Bring It On Down (live)
Creation CRESCD 182

Live Forever/Up In The Sky (acoustic)/Cloudburst/Supersonic (live)
Creation CRESCD 185

Cigarettes And Alcohol/I Am The Walrus (live)/Listen Up/Fade Away
Creation CRESCD 190

Whatever/(It's Good To) Be Free/Half The World Away/Slide Away
Creation CRESCD 195

Some Might Say/Talk Tonight/Acquiesce/Headshrinker
Creation CRESCD 204

Roll With It/It's Better People/Rockin' Chair/Live Forever (live at Glastonbury '95)
Creation CRESCD 212

Wonderwall/Round Are Way/The Swamp Song/The Master Plan
Creation CRESCD 215

Don't Look Back In Anger/Step Out/Underneath The Sky/Cum On Feel The Noize
Creation CRESCD 221

ALBUMS
Definitely Maybe
Rock'n'Roll Star/Shakermaker/Live Forever/Up In The Sky/Columbia/Supersonic/Bring It On Down/Cigarettes And Alcohol/Digsy's Dinner/Slide Away/Married With Children/Sad Song (vinyl only)
Creation CRED CD 169

(What's The Story) Morning Glory
Hello/Roll With It/Wonderwall/Don't Look Back In Anger/Hey Now/Some Might Say/Cast No Shadow/She's Electric/Morning Glory/Champagne Supernova
Creation CRED CD 189

100% UNOFFICIAL

FACT FILE GUIGSY

100%
UNOFFICIAL

PAUL McGUIGAN

BIRTHDATE:
9 May 1971

BIRTHPLACE:
Manchester

STARSIGN:
Taurus

DISTINGUISHING FEATURE:
Happy attitude

NICKNAME:
Guigsy

INSTRUMENTS:
Bass guitar

PREVIOUS EXPERIENCE:
Formed Rain with Bonehead

INFLUENCES AND IDOLS:
Paul McCartney, even though he
admits he can't play like him – yet!

THE PRICE OF FAME:
None – he's rarely recognised

LEGENDARY FOR:
Saying very little

BIGGEST HEADLINE:
Quitting a US tour through 'nervous
exhaustion'

IF OASIS ENDED TOMORROW...
He'd help out at Bonehead's studio

QUOTE UNQUOTE:
'I think cos we've known each other
for so long there's always going to
be that bond between us. Basically,
we're all here just thinking how
fantastic it all is. I love it.'

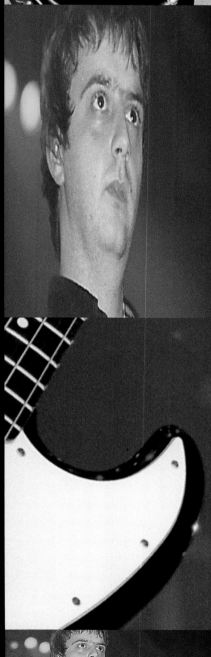

GREATEST

R egardless of how great their records are, Oasis will surely go down in rock history as one of the top live bands of all time. The songs Noel Gallagher writes are made to be played, and nothing gives the Famous Five more pleasure than doing just that.

The band's short but incident-packed career has seen them play some memorable gigs, ranging from their first to just 40 people at Manchester's Boardwalk to the massive 1996 outdoor festivals to upwards of 39,000 people. Here's a resumé of the highlights so far.

GLASTONBURY JUNE 1995

The Glastonbury Festival had turned into an annual highlight of the British rock calendar by the time Oasis were invited to play in the summer of 1995. Yet though the audience was bigger than any they'd played to date, and it was just after Noel's birthday (a fact that led to much community singing) the band didn't think they put in their usual top performance.

'I think we froze a bit,' said Noel. 'I know I did, personally. Halfway through the gig I thought we didn't really want to be there.' On the first chorus in 'Acquiesce', the

HOWS ON EARTH

lighting man turned the lights on the crowd, leaving Noel, just about to chip in with the chorus, temporarily speechless. 'I could just see these faces as far as the eye could see…'

His final verdict, 'We just didn't get it together somehow. We could have been a lot better' certainly wasn't shared by the majority. Expectations had been high…and for 99 per cent of those there (ie those not on the stage) had been fulfilled.

EARLS COURT NOVEMBER 1995

Acclaimed as the biggest indoor gigs in Britain at the time, Oasis faced playing at aircraft-hangar-like Earls Court with a mixture of pride and trepidation. They even got some scooters to run about the vast hall on, adding a little humour to proceedings.

This was stadium rock – so much so, in fact, that lighters were seen to be waved during 'Wonderwall'. 'Put 'em away,' growled Noel. 'You're not at Elton John.' But secretly he must have been proud. The first night at Earls Court put him at his ease, and from then on it was plain sailing.

'I used to get really nervous about going onstage and stuff, but now it's like, if you can pull that off, man! I even surprised meself with how good it was and how good we all played.

'So now we do these big gigs to tens of thousands of people and we might as well play in our own front room, man, because we're just totally at ease with it. Earls Court was a mad weekend. It's weird when you're in a place that big, but there was still a good atmosphere.'

Bono from U2 was spotted at Earls Court, and Noel saw him again in Paris. Checking out the opposition? Maybe – because Oasis on this form were a match for any band.

MAINE ROAD APRIL 1996

The Gallagher brothers' love affair with Manchester City FC has been well documented, so it was a dream come true when they hired the hallowed turf to play two of the biggest home-town gigs in history. 'A load of the Manchester City players have been to our gigs,' Noel explained. 'And we got a fax off Francis Lee when "Some Might Say" went to Number 1. There's a box in the new stand at Maine Road and it's going to be called the Oasis Hospitality Suite.'

The brothers' affection for City went well with their reputation as underdogs: United, with Cantona, Giggs and co, were well on their way to the second double in three years, while the less popular 'light blues' were to be relegated from the top flight in disgrace. Indeed, the 40,000 Oasis attracted to Maine Road that April weekend in 1996 was considerably in excess of what the team had been gathering! Touts were selling £17.50 tickets for £200-plus, and once inside no-one was asking for refunds.

Both shows at Maine Road were videotaped and recorded for release to the Christmas market as *There And Then*.

KNEBWORTH AUGUST 1996

The support acts alone for these two open-air gigs at Knebworth ran like a who's-who of Brit-pop – the Bootleg Beatles, the

Chemical Brothers, Ocean Colour Scene, the Manic Street Preachers, the Prodigy and the Charlatans were among the groups to support Oasis.

The celebrity count over the weekend was higher than at any gig that year. Supermodels Kate Moss and Helena Christiansen rubbed shoulderpads with actress Anna Friel of *Brookside* fame, while other pop stars spying on the main attraction ranged from fellow Mancunians Mick Hucknall and M People to Pulp mainman Jarvis Cocker…not to mention lesser celebs like Shampoo and Ant and Dec!

New songs on display included 'Gettin' Better Man' and 'My Big Mouth'. Interestingly, these were notable by their absence when Radio 1 broadcast the second night live in case bootleggers taped them and made a killing: cleverly, the broadcast then reverted to back-up tapes of the earlier night playing previously released songs. No acoustic section from Noel this time, though: was it the size of the crowd or that Liam didn't like hanging round?

Then it was on to Balloch Castle, Loch Lomond, bringing the total played to in the six open-air gigs to an estimated 330,000.

OASIS GIGS – THE AMAZING FACTS!

■ Ticket-sale phonelines once the 1996 gigs had been organised were so great that two telephone exchanges were put out of action!

■ The length of cabling used at each gig, if laid end to end, would reach from Earls Court to Maine Road and then on to Knebworth!

■ When returning to Manchester for the weekend gigs, the band booked in at several hotels to fool the press…then cancelled and stayed in Cheshire!

■ Maine Road took just three hours to sell out – twice – to become the fastest-selling stadium concerts in rock history.

100% UNOFFICIAL

BOYS *IN THE* BAN

L isten to any Oasis record you choose and it's clear to anyone with fully functioning ears that there are five musicians all contributing to the wall of sound we've come to love and appreciate. Yet with two charismatic characters like Liam and Noel in the band, it's inevitable the 'other three' will have to live in their shadow.

Happily, that's something they've learned to live with. 'Everyone's obviously going to just write about the Gallaghers,' says Bonehead, 'and we don't mind. But it is a group and we're all involved. I think 'cos we've known each other for so long there's always going to be that bond between us.'

It's a bond that's lasted throughout the 1990s, whatever fame and fortune has brought. The only change in the line-up to date came in 1995 when drummer Tony McCarroll was replaced by Alan White – and that caused Noel grief at first. 'He's a better musician than I am…which naffs me off,' said the guitar man of the tub-thumper. But he quickly mellowed. 'He does it all in one take, do you know what I mean? Alan White, he's alright – as he's now known.'

The story behind Alan's recruitment is somewhat surreal. In fact, when he got the crucial telephone call from Noel, Alan admits he was so stunned he was 'waiting for Jeremy Beadle to walk in.' His mum took the call and said 'It's Noel Gally…Gally-something…', explaining that 'He sounded Northern, like someone out of *Coronation Street*.'

Alan picked himself up off the floor and agreed to meet Noel in a café. The two immediately hit it off, to such an extent that Alan wasn't even asked to audition. He was in! Of course, he had the advantage of brother Steve being the long-time drummer for Paul Weller's band. And Weller, as we all know, is a god around the Gallagher household. They all grew up on the Jam, and to have the

D

brother of the 'Modfather's drummer was a dream come true.

Unlike the Gallagher brothers, true blue Manchester City fans, South Londoner Alan supports Charlton Athletic. His ambition is to use his double bass drum on an Oasis track, but fears the brothers will give him terminal stick for being a 'muso' (band slang for a serious musician). One day, Alan, one day…

The dynamic duo White joined forces with consisted of two Pauls, rhythm guitarist Arthurs and bassist McGuigan. To solve any confusion, the man with six strings rejoices in the name of Bonehead and his bass-playing pal 'Guigsy'. Note the spelling – anyone calling him Giggsy after the Manchester United winger will get a piece of Noel's mind!

Bonehead, who owes his nickname to his thinning thatch, was once a plasterer – the room on the cover of 'Definitely Maybe' is all his own work. He's married with a daughter, named Lucy (Noel is her godfather) and according to Noel is the most 'laddish' member of the band. 'He's like Peter Sellers and Rigsby combined, with less morals than either of them – he's just *outrageous*.'

Guigsy is rather more serious and sensitive: in fact, when the pressure of stardom got too much he temporarily retired from the band. Yet such is the 'all for one, and one for all' spirit that there was never any question of him being replaced. 'We'd been playing for two years without a break and it just kind of got on top of me,' he explained, adding 'You forget how brilliant it is to be in Oasis until you stop doing it.'

That month off, he later revealed, was 'the most boring of my life. The doctor told me I had to eat loads of vegetables. Trouble is, I *hate* vegetables.' No matter what the tabloids might say, the Oasis trio furthest from the spotlight are a long way from vegetating – musically speaking, in fact, they're chips off the old block!

OASIS SUPERQU

1

Which fashion item's sales shot up by an unprecedented 20 per cent since Oasis started wearing them?
a Jockey shorts
b Duffel coats
c Beanie hats

2

Which Manchester band gave Liam his first concert experience?
a Simply Red
b The Freshies
c Stone Roses

3

About what did Noel describe himself as 'a bit like Imelda Marcos was with shoes'?
a Jackets
b Guitars
c Records

4

Which Oasis single contained the bonus track 'Cum On Feel The Noize'?
a 'Supersonic'
b 'Shakermaker'
c 'Don't Look Back In Anger'

5

Which star did Noel once meet on the street and invite him to his birthday party, much against his better judgement?
a Morrissey
b Suggs
c Simon Le Bon

6

Which single did Liam refuse to make a video for?
a 'Some Might Say'
b 'Whatever'
c 'Shakermaker'

7

Which make of guitar does Bonehead use almost exclusively?
a Epiphone
b Fender
c Gretsch

THE MEGA-FAN CHALLENGE

Z

So you're an Oasis know-all, eh? Born in Manchester, lived in Burnage, support City and have every band member's ex-directory telephone number? Well come and have a go at this tough 20-question quiz...if you think you're hard enough!

100% UNOFFICIAL

8
Which singer did Liam once compare himself to favourably!?
a Pavarotti
b Mick Jagger
c Boyzone's Ronan

9
Which quietly spoken band member once explained 'I only do interviews with football magazines'?
a Alan
b Guigsy
c Bonehead

10
Which of these groups has never supported Oasis?
a Bootleg Beatles
b Kula Shaker
c Blur

11
How many singles had Oasis released before hitting the Number 1 slot with 'Some Might Say'?
a 3
b 4
c 5

? ? ? ? ? ? ? ?

12

Whose old man apparently *is* a dustman – and according to Noel, 'Blur will probably try and steal him'?
a Alan
b Guigsy
c Bonehead

13

With whom did Noel duet on TV's *The White Room*?
a Elvis Costello
b Paul Weller
c Peter Andre

14

Which pop know-it-all once said: 'Until six months ago, I thought Blondie were French'?
a Liam
b Noel
c Bonehead

15

What is the instrumental Oasis have typically opened their show with?
a 'Apache'
b 'Swamp Song'
c 'Green Onions'

16

Which group did Noel nearly join, replacing Bernard Butler?
a Blur
b Ocean Colour Scene
c Suede

17

When Oasis reissued all their singles in box-set form, what did those boxes resemble?
a Cornflake packets
b Cigarette packets
c Duffel bags

18
Which of these groups is/was not a real Oasis tribute outfit?
a The Gallaghers
b No Way Sis
c Mad For It

19
Which group did Liam's loved one Patsy Kensit once sing with?
a No Doubt
b Eighth Wonder
c The Maisonettes

20
Which Oasis single became the highest ever new entry into the US chart, appearing at Number 21?
a 'Supersonic'
b 'Roll With It'
c 'Wonderwall'

HOW YOU SCORED
0-7
Sorry, squire – your vision is extremely Blurred! You've been around the (Ocean Colour) Scene for far too short a time to have sorted your Liams from your Noels – and it's high time you learned... We recommend another in-depth read of this book, a diet of wall-to-(wonder)wall Oasis tunes, and a weekend in Manchester. If the band aren't around, meet 'em at Maine Road!

8-14
You're clearly mad for it – but don't get too cocky just yet! There's a lot you still need to learn about the ways of the biggest band in Brit-pop before you can claim to be a super-fan. Keep on studying Oasis sound and style, and you'll have no problems holding up your end in any argument. Manchester rules okay!

15 or over
Okay, Noel – you've been rumbled! If your surname isn't Gallagher, however, consider yourself a real Oasis know-all. Your knowledge of Manchester's top band bar none is just as exceptional as their music, and as long as you keep out of trouble and don't punch out the paparazzi there's a bright future ahead.

? ? ? ? ? ? ? ? ? ?

FACT FILE ALAN

ALAN WHITE

BIRTHDATE:
26 May 1972

BIRTHPLACE:
London

STARSIGN:
Gemini

DISTINGUISHING FEATURE:
Looks like his brother, Paul Weller's drummer

NICKNAME:
Whitey

INSTRUMENTS:
Drums, drums and more drums

PREVIOUS EXPERIENCE:
First band Starclub, plus countless sessions

INFLUENCES AND IDOLS:
Brother Steve, 'the Guv'nor'

THE PRICE OF FAME:
Being followed round the supermarket in Lewisham where he used to work – 'a bit of a buzz'

LEGENDARY FOR:
Pure musical ability

BIGGEST HEADLINE:
Joining Oasis on the eve of their second album

IF OASIS ENDED TOMORROW...
He'd become an in-demand session musician

QUOTE UNQUOTE:
'I'm going to get back into doing my Latin and samba stuff, a bit more technical stuff than I've been doing with Oasis. I really enjoy the straightforward stuff, but it does get a bit frustrating...'

WHITE

MAD ▼ FOR IT!

LIAM
LOVE AND LOUTISHNESS

hen it comes to rock'n'roll, the press have always needed a fear figure – someone who personifies all the dangers of the rock'n'roll lifestyle. For a brief moment it was Elvis...then came Rolling Stone Mick Jagger, who even ended up banged up in jail on a trivial charge. In the 1970s Johnny Rotten came along in full punk warpaint to scare the (bondage) pants off parents, while the 1980s – full of Live Aid-style compassion – only sparked into life with the arrival of Guns N'Roses.

Then came Oasis...and Liam Gallagher in particular. His extrovert, couldn't give a you-know-what antics guaranteed headlines even before he opened his mouth. And even though his lifestyle was often wild enough to get up Noel's nose – most notably when he failed to show up for a Jools Holland TV slot, leaving big brother to handle vocals – he's survived to tell the tale.

Not only that, he's managed to get his love life into the world's headlines courtesy of the highest of high-profile relationships with singer turned film star Patsy Kensit. Painted by some as the Yoko Ono to Liam's Lennon, allegedly intent on separating her beloved from the rest of 'ver lads', she had two marriages to rock stars behind her – and early 1997 saw the global press on their doorstep with rumours of Number Three.

Patsy had, in order, been the 'other half' to Big Audio Dynamite drummer Dan Donovan and Simple Minds singer Jim Kerr before throwing in her lot with the Oasis wild man. Given Kerr had previously been 'Mr Chrissie Hynde' (of Pretenders fame), plus the fact that she'd been seeing Kinks singer Ray Davies, there was almost a book to be written about rock'n'roll relationships. Liam and Patsy eventually wed in a 15-minute ceremony at London's Westminster Registry Office on 7th April, Liam attracting headlines by banning his father's name from the wedding certificate.

While Noel – the older Gallagher by six years, remember – had traditionally preferred to be in a steady relationship Liam was a 'love 'em and leave 'em' type. He'd always had a thing for pop stars, and those he was alleged to have romanced included Lisa Moorish, Berri of 'Sunshine After The Rain' fame and 'French bird' Sandrine de La Plage. His attitude, one of a fun-loving bachelor keen to avoid being tied down, could be summed up in the quote: 'I've just split up with a girl but I didn't love her, so it doesn't really matter, does it?'

One-time *Word* presenter Amanda de Cadenet was said to have attracted Liam's roving eye…but when, as rumour had it, Paula Yates took an interest in his welfare the younger Gallagher ran a mile and locked himself in a bathroom. C'mon, Liam – she was only making conversation!

But Patsy was different, even though their romance had its ups and downs, its ons and offs. By March 1996, just months after their affair began, things were already serious enough for her to fly the Atlantic to be with him as Oasis tried to conquer the States. And when she guested on Chris Evans' TV show, she all but forgot about the new film she was supposed to be plugging to spill some beans about their publicity-attracting romance.

It all seemed a far cry from the early days of Oasis, where Liam – maybe seeking

100% UNOFFICIAL

'Everything just went mad. People were smashing bottles and throwing things all over the place. At one point, someone opened a window and started to lob everything out. I woke up the next morning, looked out of the window and the car park was full of bedrooms. It was a laugh.'

These days, though, instead of smashing up rooms you're more likely to see Liam sloping off to his local convenience store for a pint of milk before returning to hearth and home in the house he shares with Patsy. Near neighbours in the secluded and highly exclusive London suburb they've made their home include Sir Paul McCartney and George Michael.

Oasis have taken their foot off the touring accelerator in favour of studio work – just like the Beatles did in 1966 – which has given him a chance to take stock, reassess the situation and come to grips with the great rewards and the pressures fame has brought.

Until you've had the press looking through your dustbin for fascinating finds, or had a barrage of flashguns go off in

security as he struggled to come to terms with fame – partied in public on numerous occasions. The legendary ferry incident was just one example. 'I like drinking. I love it. I'm into it. I'm not saying I'm proud of what happened but…that's the way we are, the way I am. Rock'n'roll is about being yourself. And I went on that boat, I had a drink, I had too much beer and I got in a fight and that was it.'

While most stars crave attention, yet hate the off-stage price of fame, Liam has also had to come to terms with the fact that though he's Oasis's singer and frontman, Noel writes the songs. 'I'm more the band than he is,' he once snarled. '*I'm* the talent.' But he's had to accept that some of the credit will go elsewhere, and that any songs he wants to write will have to be saved for outside projects like John Squire's Seahorses.

The pressures of life in the media spotlight that build up day by day inevitably come to a head, and rock bands have traditionally let off steam by 'redecorating' the hotels they stay in while on tour. Liam has enjoyed his share of that too, as he explained in 1994.

your face as you open the curtains, you can't truly understand the day to day life of a superstar. When you get up on stage, you expect exposure as a matter of course. But 365 days a year is a bit much...and if paparazzi pictures show Liam expressing his displeasure with the occasional obscene gesture, then ask yourself – wouldn't *you*?

All the facts seem to suggest that Liam Gallagher is – wait for it – maturing. Yes, we'll see more bad behaviour, like at the 1996 Brits, and on-stage he's likely to be pacing about like the caged animal he's always taken delight in imitating. But with a stable home environment behind him (don't forget, life in Burnage as a kid wasn't always the most harmonious), we can expect him to save his energies for the public that adores him, not waste it on pressmen paid by the scandal-packed column inch.

So when it comes down to the $64,000 question – does Liam Gallagher truly deserve his wild man of rock tag? – the jury must remain out...for now.

BIGGE
THE BE

One of Oasis's most famous anthems is 'Live Forever' – yet, as we all know, pop groups don't tend to last nearly that long. Even the Beatles only managed an eight-year recording career before simply finding they couldn't stand the sight of each other. So what will the future hold for Manchester's finest?

'If the band split up,' Liam told reporters in 1994, 'I wouldn't stop, I'd go on. I wouldn't just be a singer, I'd carry on as a guitarist/singer like Lennon. It's like "Live Forever" – if you get to know yourself, and you get to know your spirit, your spirit will live forever.'

In contrast, Noel has never seen Oasis going on indefinitely – or even anything like it. 'Three albums and that's it,' he said in 1995. 'I don't think I can do any more with Oasis after that. I think a band like us will have run our course. There's only so

many anthems you can write...you've got to step up and change or step back a bit and change. I don't know for sure, but I'd say the next one will be the last one.' So what would he do then? 'Sell shoes, probably.'

The Beatles all came from Liverpool, but got involved in Eastern religion, politics and other distractions that made them much less of a unit than once they were. People have pointed to Liam's relationship with actress Patsy Kensit as being similar to John Lennon and Yoko Ono – arguably the biggest single factor in the Beatles' split. Yet they underestimate the family bonds between the brothers, and their affection for the boys in the band – an affinity that's a lot more than skin deep.

It's a fact of life that the one thing rooting Oasis in reality despite the head-turning success they've enjoyed is the tight

RTHAN
ATLES?

connections between its members. As Noel puts it, 'I'm Bonehead's daughter's godfather, right, and I'm Liam Gallagher's brother, and I'm Guigsy's best friend, and I'm Alan White's best friend. We are a family.'

But while Oasis intend to stay together, side trips are most definitely on the menu. There have already been collaborations between Noel and other groups: most successful was 1996's chart-topping 'Setting Sun' with the Chemical Brothers, while Liam's written at least one song with former Stone Rose John Squire. Other collaborations are likely, even though a song Noel wrote with chief Lemonhead Evan Dando, 'Purple Parallelogram', was axed when poised for single release because Noel didn't think it was that good. Here's someone whose quality control is clearly never going to be compromised!

The one thing Noel doesn't plan to do, though, is go solo. 'This is my first band, my first rock'n'roll experience and it'll be my last,' he insists. 'I mean that from the bottom of my heart.'

So if all continues as at present and Oasis stay together through 1998 and into the next century, can we expect them to be the new Beatles? Liam has no doubts. 'I think we'll be the most important band in the world,' he laughs, expletives deleted. 'If time is on our side and no-one dies, then we'll be the new Beatles. We'll mean just as much because Noel's written about 200 songs nobody's ever heard and every one of them is a classic. We're way ahead.'

Noel, of course, has already collaborated with a real-life Beatle – bassist Paul (now Sir Paul) McCartney, when they recorded as the Smokin' Mojo Filters for the War Child charity. 'I was terrified when I met him,'

Noel admitted. 'I didn't have anything to say. But it was good when he taught me the chords to "Come Together".'

The reason Noel holds the Fab Four in such high regard is their ability to write concise, catchy three-minute pop songs like 'Ticket To Ride' – his all-time favourite. Yet the Beatles progressed from that to 'Sgt Pepper' and their psychedelic period – so will we see Oasis doing likewise? Fact is, there's already Kula Shaker operating in that area, while even one-time rivals Blur have shown more of a leaning towards the late-Beatles sound with their 1997 album. More likely is a move towards social comment, which with the Fabs was definitely the province of one John Ono Lennon.

Though Noel believes he wouldn't have got on with John at all, it doesn't stop him loving the late great Beatle's songs. 'They meant a real lot to me. I don't care about songwriters, all I care about is the songs.' So much in fact that he admits to borrowing some of the lyrics for 'Don't Look Back In Anger' from an unreleased tape of Lennon starting to record his memoirs shortly before his 1980 assassination. 'He's going on about "trying to start a revolution from me bed, because they said the brains I had went to my head." Thank you, I'll take that.'

It's no surprise then that Noel compares every song he writes to the Beatles – and admits he's got 'semi-close once or twice…the thing is, they got there before me. If I'd been born at the same time as John Lennon, I'd have been up there. Well, I'd definitely have been better than Gerry and the Pacemakers!'

But when the end comes, Oasis will go out with heads held high, Noel reveals. 'We will sit back with our consciences clear that we never lied to anyone. That's why I will slag my record company off in public, I'll slag Liam off in public and he'll slag me off in public. We won't hold it all in, because if we're people's favourite band they should know what that band's about.'

When music history records the impact of Oasis, they can look back at the likes of Ocean Colour Scene, Kula Shaker and the Verve as acts who followed the trail they blazed. Living forever may be impossible, even for the brothers Gallagher – but the music they, Bonehead, Guigsy and Alan White have given the world looks set to echo for some while yet. And that's definitely…*not* maybe!